An Outline Guide for The Calvary Road

Student's Edition

By
Pastor Jeremy Markle

For
The Calvary Road
by
Roy Hession

WALKING IN THE WORD
MINISTRIES

Pastor/Missionary Jeremy Markle
www.walkinginthewordministries.net

An
Outline Guide
for
The Calvary Road
Student's Edition

This outline study was compiled by
Pastor Jeremy Markle
for Roy Hession's book,
The Calvary Road
© CLC Publishers, Fort Washington, PA 19034
2010.
Used by permission from the Roy Hession Trust,
Scotland.

Unless otherwise noted,
all Scripture quotations are from the King James Version.

Published by Walking in the WORD Ministries
www.walkinginthewordministries.net

Printed in the United States of America

ISBN: 978-0692519479

Preface

This outline guide was written to enhance your ability to understand, remember, and apply the important spiritual truths shared by Roy Hession in his book, *The Calvary Road*. After reading each chapter, you can review its content by filling in the blanks, considering the additional passages provided, and answering the reflection and application questions. Throughout this outline guide there are a few special features to help you focus on the truths being taught:

Text Quotations – Both long and short quotations that are taken directly from the text are provided to emphasize the spiritual truths being taught.

Scripture Quotations and References – Numerous Scripture quotations and verse references from the text are given in the outline to encourage personal consideration of the authority of God's Word for each subject.

Additional Scripture Quotations – Additional Scripture quotations not mentioned in the text have been quoted in boxes entitled "Additional Truth," which enhance the subject matter.

Additional Scripture References – Additional Scripture references not mentioned in the text have been printed in italics throughout the outline, which can be looked up to enhance the understanding of the subject matter.

Reflection and Application Questions – Reflection and Application questions are provided throughout the outline to encourage personal and practical application of what has been learned.

This outline guide is published in two editions. The Teacher's Edition has each blank filled in to help the teacher during public instruction. The Student's Edition has blanks that can be filled either in a group setting or individually during personal study.

It is my deepest desire that this outline guide will be a practical help by directing your spiritual eyes to Jesus Christ through the important spiritual truths found in *The Calvary Road*.

Pastor Jeremy Markle

Content

Brokenness. 7

Cups Running Over. 17

The Way of Fellowship. 27

The Highway of Holiness. 37

The Dove and the Lamb. 51

Revival in the Home. 63

The Mote and the Beam. 73

Are You Willing to Be a Servant?. 81

The Power of the Blood of the Lamb. 93

Protesting Our Innocence?. 105

The Calvary Road
Outline Guide

Chapter 1

Brokenness

Brokenness

"We want to be very simple in this matter of revival. Revival is just the life of the Lord Jesus poured into human hearts. Jesus is always victorious. In heaven they are praising Him all the time for His victory. What ever may be our experience of failure and barrenness, He is never defeated. His power is to get into a right relationship with Him and we shall see His power being demonstrated in our hearts and lives and service, and His victorious life will fill us and overflow through us to others. And that is revival in its essence."

> **Additional Truth**
>
> **Psalm 51:17**
> *17 The sacrifices of God are a broken spirit:*
> *a broken and a contrite heart, O God,*
> *thou wilt not despise.*

Galatians 2:20
20 I am crucified with Christ: nevertheless I live;
yet not I, but Christ liveth in me:
and the life which I now live in the flesh
I live by the faith
of the Son of God, who loved me,
and gave himself for me.

I. Brokenness begins revival (the victorious life)

A. Brokenness is ...

1. P roud self

2. H _____

"It is being 'Not I, but Christ,' and a 'C' is a bent 'I.' The Lord Jesus cannot live in us fully and reveal Himself through us until the proud self within us is broken ... In other words, it is dying to self and self-attitude."

B.   Brokeness eliminates ...
   1.   J_____ ones self
   2.   W_____ one's own way
   3.   S+and up for one's rights
   4.   S_____ one's own glory

C.   Brokeness implements ...
   "... bows its head to God's will ..."
   1.   ' Admitting one's w_____
   2.   Giving up it's own w_____
   3.   Surrendering its r_____
   4.   Discarding its own g_____

Reflection & Application

✎What are some ways that brokennes can be displayed at home, work, church, etc.?

_____

_____

_____

II.   The evidence for the need for brokenness
   A.   "I am t_____" to live the Christian life
   B.   "I am d_____" service for the Lord
   C.   I_____
   D.   E_____
   E.   R_____
   F.   C_____

G. W_____

H. H_____ ... with others

I. U_____ with others

J. S____

K. S_____

L. R_____

"... the fruit of the Spirit ... is the complete antithesis of the hard, unbroken spirit within us ..."

Galatians 5:22-26

22 But the fruit of the Spirit is love, joy, peace, longsuffering,
gentleness, goodness, faith,
23 Meekness, temperance:
against such there is no law.
24 And they that are Christ's
have crucified the flesh
with the affections and lusts.
25 If we live in the Spirit,
let us also walk in the Spirit.
26 Let us not be desirous of vain glory,
provoking one another, envying one another.

"Being broken is both God's work and ours. He brings His pressure to bear, but we have to make the choice ... We can stiffen our necks and refuse to repent, or we can bow the head and say, 'yes Lord.' Brokenness in daily experience is simply the response of humility to the conviction of God ... And this can be very costly, when we see all the yielding of rights and selfish interests that this will involve, and the confessions and restitutions that may be sometimes necessary"

Reflection & Application

✎What are some ways of living for self which you need to repent of?

_____

_____

_____

III. The example of Jesus Christ's brokenness

"The willingness of Jesus to be broken for us is the all compelling motive in our being broken too."

Philippians 2:5-8
5 Let this mind be in you,
which was also in Christ Jesus:
6 Who, being in the form of God
thought it not robbery to be equal with God:
7 But made himself of no reputation,
and took upon him
the form of a servant,
and was made in the likeness of men:
8 And being found in fashion as a man,
he humbled himself,
and became obedient unto death,
even the death of the cross.

   A.   He was in the form of a s_____
      II Corinthians 4:5
      1.   Servant of G_____
      2.   Servant of m_____

B.   He had no r_____
*Psalm 22:6

C.   He was reviled and did not r_____ again
"Willing to let men tread on Him and not retaliate or defend himself."
*I Peter 2:21-24

D.   He became man's s_____ by bearing their sins
*Romans 5:6-8

Psalm 22:6

*6 But I am a worm, and no man;
a reproach of men, and despised of the people.*

"The snake rears itself up and hisses and tries to strike back–a true picture of self. But a worm offers no resistance, it allows you to do what you like with it ... Jesus was willing to become just that for us–a worm and no man ... And He now calls us to take our rightful place as worms for Him and with Him."

"Lord, bend that proud and stiffnecked I,
Help me to bow the head and die;
Beholding Him on Calvary,
Who bowed His head for me."

Additional Truth

John 19:30
*30 When Jesus therefore
had received the vinegar,
he said, It is finished:
and he bowed his head,
and gave up the ghost.*

Additional Truth

II Corinthians 5:14-15
*14 For the love of Christ constraineth us;
because we thus judge,
that if one died for all, then were all dead:
15 And that he died for all,
that they which live
should not henceforth live unto themselves,
but unto him which died for them,
and rose again.*

IV. The continual brokenness
    A.   Brokenness begins with the i____ dying to self
        "When God first shows these things ..."
        II Corinthians 7:8-11

B. Brokennes continues with a c_____ dying to self

"For only so can the Lord Jesus be revealed constantly through us."

*II Corinthians 4:10-11

1. Giving God my ...
    a. P_____
    b. T_____
    c. M_____
    d. P_____

2. Giving others ... for God's sake
    a. The r_____ away

    "It will mean a constant yieldedness to those around us, for our yieldedness to God is measured by our yieldedness to man."

    b. H_____

    "... everyone who tries and vexes us, is God's way of breaking us, so that there is a yet deeper channel in us for the Life of Christ."

"You see, the only life that pleases God and that can be victorious is His life–never our life, no matter how hard we try. But inasmuch as our self-centered life is the exact opposite of His, we can never be filled with His life unless we are prepared for God to bring our life constantly to death. And in that we must co-operate by our moral choice."

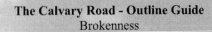

Reflection & Application

✎Are you committed to live the victorious Christian life by letting Jesus Christ live through you?

_____

The Calvary Road
Outline Guide

Chapter 2

Cups Running Over

Cups Running Over

"Revival itself is being absolutely filled to overflowing with the Holy Spirit, and that is victorious living ... All we have to do is to present our empty, broken self and let Him fill and keep filled. Andrew Murray says, 'Just as water ever seeks and fills the lowest place, so the moment God finds you abased and empty, His glory and power flow in.' The picture that has made things simple and clear to so many of us is that of the human heart as a cup, which we hold out to Jesus, longing that He might fill it with the Water of Lie. Jesus is pictured as bearing the golden water pot with the Water of Life. As He passes by He looks into our cup, and if it is clean, He fills it to overflowing with the Water of Life. And as Jesus is always passing by, the cup can be always running over."

Additional Truth

John 4:6-16 (10-11)
10 Jesus answered and said unto her,
If thou knewest the gift of God,
and who it is that saith to thee,
Give me to drink; thou wouldest have asked of him,
and he would have given thee living water.
11 The woman saith unto him,
Sir, thou hast nothing to draw with,
and the well is deep:
from whence then hast thou that living water?

Additional Truth

John 4:6-16 (13-15)
13 Jesus answered and said unto her,
Whosoever drinketh of this water shall thirst again:
14 But whosoever drinketh of the water
that I shall give him shall never thirst;
but the water that I shall give him
shall be in him a well of water springing up
into everlasting life.
15 The woman saith unto him,
Sir, give me this water, that I thirst not,
neither come hither to draw.

I. **The one thing that prevents spiritual filling: <u>S   </u>**

"Anything that springs from self, however small it may be, is sin."

- A. S_____
- B. S_____
- C. S_____
- D. S_____
  - 1. In b_____
  - 2. In C_____ work
- E. S_____
- F. T_____
- G. R_____
- H. S_____
- I. S_____
- J. R_____
- K. W_____
- L. F_____

20

"... all are sin and make our cups unclean. But all of them were put into that other cup, which the Lord Jesus shrank from momentarily in Gathsemane, but which he drank to the dregs at calvary–the cup of our sin. And if we will allow him to show us that is in our cups and then give it to Him, He will cleans them in the precious blood that still flows form sin. That does not mean mere cleansing from the guilt of sin, nor even from the stain of sin–though thank God both of these are true–but from the sin itself, whatever it may be. And as He cleanses our cups, so He fills them to overflowing with His Holy Spirit"
Psalm 119:9, II Timothy 2:19-21, I John 1:7-10

Reflection & Application

✎What are some common ways in which our spiritual vessel can become dirty throughout a day?

_____

_____

_____

II. The source for constant cleansing: B_____ of Christ

"Suppose you have let the Lord Jesus cleanse your cup and have trusted Him to fill it to overflowing, then something comes along–a touch of envy or temper. What happens? Your cup becomes dirty and it ceases to overflow. And if we are constantly being defeated in this way, then our cup is never overflowing."

"If we are to know continuous revival, we must learn the way to keep our cups clean."

Additional Truth

I John 1:7, 9
7 But if we walk in the light, as he is in the light,
we have fellowship one with another,
and the blood of Jesus Christ his Son
cleanseth us from all sin.
9 If we confess our sins,
he is faithful and just to forgive us our sins,
and to cleanse us from all unrighteousness.

A.   The constant g_____ back to Calvary

"... learn afresh the power of the blood of Jesus to cleanse moment by moment from the beginnings of sin ... And the more you trust the blood of Jesus in this way, the less will you even have these reactions."

B.   The constant b_____ over sin

"Suppose we are irritated by certain traits in someone. It is not enough just to take our reactions of irritation to Calvary. We must first be broken; that is, we must yield to God over the whole question and accept that person and his ways as His will for us ... and when we have been cleansed from sin, let us not keep mourning over it, let us not be occupied with ourselves. But let us look up to our victorious Lord and praise Him that He is still victorious."

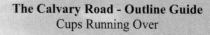

Reflection & Application

✎How can you quickly go back to Calvary when sin enters your life throughout the day?

_____

III. The test (referee) of a dirty life: P_____

"Everything that disturbs the peace of God in our hearts is sin, no matter how small it is, and no matter how little like sin it may at first appear to be."

Colossians 3:15
15 And let the peace of God rule in your hearts,
to the which also ye are called in one body;
and be ye thankful.

A.   When peace is d_____, sin has entered our life
   Psalm 32:3-4

B.   When peace is r_____; true confession, cleansing, and correction has taken place
   Psalm 32:1-11, 51:1-19

   1.   Confession - "Let us s____ immediately, ask God to show us what is wrong ..."
      Psalm 139:23-24

   2.   Cleansing - "... p___ by faith the sin He shows us under the blood of Jesus ..."

   3.   Correction - "... peace will be r_____ and we shall go on our way with our cups running over."

23

"If, however, God does not give us His peace, it will be because we are not really broken. Perhaps we have yet to say 'sorry' to somebody else as well as to God. Or perhaps we still feel it the other person's fault ... But if we have lost our peace, it is obvious whose fault it is. We do not lose peace, it is obvious whose fault it is. We do not lose peace wit God over another person's sin, but only over our own."

Additional Truth

Proverbs 28:13
13 He that covereth his sins shall not prosper:
but whoso confesseth and forsaketh them
shall have mercy.

"Many times a day and over the smallest things we shall have to avail ourselves to the cleansing blood of Jesus, and we shall find ourselves walking the way of brokenness as never before. But Jesus will be manifested in all His loveliness and grace in that brokenness."

"Many of us, however, have neglected the referee's whistle so often and for so long that we have ceased to hear it. Days follow days and we feel we have little need of cleansing and no occasion of being broken. In that condition we are usually in a worse state than we ever imagine. It will take a great hunger for restored fellowship with god to possess our hearts before we will be willing to cry to god to show us where the blood of Jesus must be applied. He will show us, to begin with, just one thing, and it will be our obedience and brokenness on that on thing that will be the first step into revival for us."

Reflection & Application

✎What are some evidences of lost peace in your life?

_____

_____

_____

Reflection & Application

✎How can you get God's peace back in your life?

_____

_____

_____

The Calvary Road
Outline Guide

Chapter 3

The Way of Fellowship

The Way of Fellowship

"When man fell and chose to make himself, rather than God, the center of his life, the effect was not only to put man out of fellowship with God, but also out of fellowship with his fellow man ... The Fall is simply, 'We have turned every one to his own way' [Isaiah 53:6]. If I want my own way rather than God's, it is quite obvious that I shall want my own way rather than the other man's ... But a world in which each man wants his own way cannot but be a world full of tensions, barriers, suspicions, misunderstandings, clashes, and conflicts."

   *James 4:1-3

"Now the work of the Lord Jesus Christ on the cross was not only to bring men back into fellowship with God, but also into fellowship with their fellow men."

I John 2:9, 3:14-15, 4:20

2:9 He that saith he is in the light,
and hateth his brother,
is in darkness even until now.
3:14 We know that we have passed from death unto life,
because we love the brethren.
He that loveth not his brother abideth in death.
15 Whosoever hateth his brother is a murderer:
and ye know
that no murderer hath eternal life abiding in him.
4:20 If a man say, I love God, and hateth his brother,
he is a liar:
for he that loveth not his brother whom he hath seen,
how can he love God whom he hath not seen?

"Some of us have come to see how utterly connected a man's relationship to his fellows is with his relationship to God. Everything that comes as a barrier between us and another, be it ever so small, comes as a barrier between us and God. We have ound that where theses barriers are not put right immediately, they get thicker and thicker until we find ourselves shut off from God and our brother by what seem to be veritable brick walls. Quite obviously, if we allow new life to come to us, it will have to manifest itself by a walk of oneness with God and our brother, with nothing between."

I.   Light and D_____

"On what basis can we have real fellowship with God and our brother?

I John 1:7
7 But if we walk in the light, as he is in the light,
we have fellowship one with another,
and the blood of Jesus Christ his Son
cleanseth us from all sin.

A.   Light r_____

"When anything reproves us, shows us up as we really are–that is light."
John 3:19-21

Ephesians 5:13
13 But all things that are reproved
are made manifest by the light:
for whatsoever doth make manifest is light.

B.   Darkness h_____

"But whenever we do anything or say anything (or don't say anything) to hide what we are or what we've done–that is darkness."
Genesis 3:6-11

"Now the first effect of sin in our lives is always to make us try to hide what we are ... Sin always involves us in being unreal, pretending, duplicity, window dressing, excusing ourselves and blaming others–and we can do all that as much by our silence as by saying or doing something."

"In contrast to all this in us, verse 5 of this chapter of I john tells us that 'God is light,' that is, God is the All-revealing One, who shows up every man as he really is."

"Quite obviously, then, it is utterly impossible for us to be walking in any degree of darkness and have fellowship with God. While we are in that condition of darkness, we cannot have true fellowship with our brother either–for we are not real with him, and no one can have fellowship with an unreal person. A wall of reserve separates him and us."

Reflection & Application

✎What are some ways that we might try to coverup our sin?

_____

_____

_____

II.   The only basis for f_____

"The only basis for real fellowship with God and man is to live out in the open with both ... Spurgeon defines it in one of his sermons as 'the willingness to know and be known.'"

A.   Fellowship with G_____
Psalm 139:1-24

1.   We are w_____ to know the whole truth about ourselves

2.   We are o_____ to conviction
"We will bend the neck to the first twinges of conscience."

31

3. We will hide or excuse n _____
"Everything He shows us to be sin, we will deal with as sin ..."

"Such a walk in the light cannot but disclose sin increasingly in our lives, and we shall see things to be sin which we never thought to be such before. For that reason we might shrink from this walk, and be tempted to make for cover. But the verse goes on with the precious words, 'and the blood of Jesus Christ his Son cleanseth us from all sin.'"

B. Fellowship with m_____
1. We must be as w_____ to know the truth about ourselves from our brother as to know it from God.
2. We must be p_____ for him to hold the light to us (and we are be willing to do the same service for him) and challenge us in love about anything.
3. We must be w___ to not only know, but to be known by him for what we really are.

"That means we are not going to hide our inner selves from those with whom we ought to be in fellowship; we are not going to window-dress and put on appearances; nor are we going to whitewall and excuse ourselves. We are going to be honest about ourselves with them. We are willing to give up our spiritual privacy, pocket our pride, and risk our reputations for the sake of being open and transparent with our brethren in Christ. It means, too, that we are not going to cherish any wrong feeling

in our hearts about another, but we are first going to claim deliverance from it from God and put it right with the one concerned. As we walk this way, we shall find that we shall have fellowship with one another at an altogether new level, and we shall not love one another less, but infinitely more."
Matthew 5:23-24, 6:14-15, 18:15-22, Mark 11:25-26

Reflection & Application

✎How is a relationship of openness different from a relationship of hiding?

_____

_____

_____

III. No B_____

"We have not necessarily got to tell everybody everything about ourselves. The fundamental thing is our *attitude* ..."

A. True t_____

"Are we willing to be in the open with our brother–and be so in word when God tells us to? That is the 'armor of light'–true transparency."

B. Absolutely h_____

"But let a man begin to be absolutely honest about himself with but one other, as God guides him, and he will com to a knowledge of himself and his sins that he never had before, and he will begin to see more clearly than ever before where the redemption of Christ has got to be applied progressively to his life. This is the reason why James tells us to put ourselves under the discipline of 'confessing our faults one to another' [James 5:16]."

C. Love will f_____

"Obviously, love will flow from one to another when each is prepared to be known as the repentant sinner he is at the cross of Jesus. When the barriers are down and the masks are off, God has a chance of making us really one."
I Corinthians 13:4-8

"But there is also the added joy of knowing that in sucha fellowship we are 'safe.' No fear now that others may be thinking thoughts about us or having reactions toward us which they are hiding from us. In a fellowship which is committed to walk in the light beneath the cross, we know that if there is any thougth about us it will quickly be brought int the light, either in brokenness and confession (where there has been wrong and unlove), or else as a loving challenge, as something that we ought to know about ourselves."
I John 4:17

IV. Teams of t_____ for revival

"Jesus wants you to begin walking in the light with Him in a new way today."

A. J____ with one other–your Christian friend, the person you live with, your wife, your husband.

"Drop the mask. God has doubtless convicted you of one thing more than another that you have got to be honest with them about.

B. Get t_____ from time to time for fellowship and to share your spiritual experiences with real openness.
Hebrews 10:24-25

34

C. In complete oneness pray t_____ for others.
    Matthew 18:19-20

D. Go out as a t_____ with fresh testimony.

"God through such a fellowship will begin to work wondrously. As He saves and blesses others in this vital way, they can start to live and work as a fellowship too. As one billiard ball will move another billiard ball, so one group will set off another group, until the whole of our land is covered with new life from the risen Lord Jesus."

Reflection & Application

✎Are you committed to join with fellow believers at home and church for the purpose of revival?

_____

The Calvary Road
Outline Guide

Chapter 4

The Highway of Holiness

The Highway of Holines

Isaiah 35:8-9

8 And an highway shall be there, and a way,
and it shall be called The way of holiness;
the unclean shall not pass over it;
but it shall be for those: the wayfaring men,
though fools, shall not err therein.
9 No lion shall be there,
nor any ravenous beast shall go up thereon,
it shall not be found there;
but the redeemed shall walk there:

I.   **The H**_____

   A.   The Highway is not b_____ any of us - "... it shall be for those: the wayfaring men, though fools, shall not err therein." (8c)

   B.   The Highway is a s____ place - "No lion shall be there, nor any ravenous beast shall go up thereon." (9a)

   C.   The Highway is not traveled by the u_____ - "... unclean shall not pass over it; ..." (8b)
"This includes not only the sinner who does not know Christ as his Saviour, but the Christian who does and yet is walking in unconfessed and uncleansed sin.
Proverbs 28:13

"The only way onto the Highway is up a small, dark, forbidding hill–the Hill of Calvary. It is the sort of hill we have to climb on our hands and knees–especially our knees if we are content with our present Christian life, if we do not desire with a desperate hunger to get onto the Highway, we shall never get to our knees and thus never climb the hill."

Jeremiah 29:13
13 And ye shall seek me, and find me,
when ye shall search for me with all your heart.

Reflection & Application

✎What are some evidences of lost peace in your life?

_____

_____

_____

II. A l_____ door

"At the top of the hill, guarding the way to the Highway, stands so gaunt and grim ... the cross. There it stands, the divider of time and the divider of th men. At the foot of the cross is a low door, so low that to get through it one has to stoop and crawl through. It is the only entrance to the Highway. We must go through it if we would go any further on our way. This door is called the Door of the Broken Ones. Only the broken can enter the Highway. To be broken means to be 'not I, but Christ.'"

A. The prevention of passage: A s_____ neck (unbending and unbroken)

"There is in every one of us a proud, stiff-necked "I." The stiff neck began in the Garden of Eden when Adam and Eve, who had always bowed their heads in surrender to God's will, stiffened their necks, struck out for independence, and tried to be 'as gods'"

1. H_____ and unyielding
2. S_____ and easily hurt
3. I_____
4. E_____
5. C_____ l
6. R_____ and unforgiving
7. S_____

B. The preparation for passage: B_____

   "Before we can enter the Highway, God must bend and break that stiff-necked self, so that Chris reigns in its stead."

   1. The definition of brokenness - "to have no r_____"

      "To be broken means to have no rights before God and man. It does not mean merely surrendering my rights to Him but rather recognizing that I haven't any, except to deserve hell. It means just being nothing and having nothing that I call my own, neither time, money, possessions, nor position."

   2. The example of brokeness - Jesus Christ on the c_____

      "In order to break our wills to His, God brings us to the foot of the cross and there shows us what real brokenness is. We see those wounded hands and feet, that face of love crowned with thorns, and the we see the complete brokenness of the One who said, 'Not my will, but Thine be done,' as He drank the bitter cup of our sin to its dregs. So the way to be broken is to look on Him and realize it was our sin which nailed Him there. Then as we see the love and brokenness of the

God who died in our place, our hearts will become stangely melted and we will want to be broken for Him and we shall pray, ..."

"Oh, to be saved from myself, dear Lord,
Oh, to be lost in Thee,
Oh, that it might be no more I,
But Christ that lives in me."

Reflection & Application

✎What are some proper reactions to people and circumstances which show that you are broken before God?

_____

_____

_____

III. A c_____ choice

A. Brokenness must be a c_____ choice
"But do not let us imagine that we have to be broken only once as we go through the door. Ever after it will be a constant choice."
Galatians 2:20

B. Brokenness will be t_____ by others
"If someone hurts and slights us, we immediately have the choice of accepting the slight as a means of grace to humble us lower or we can resist it and stiffen our necks again with all the disturbance of spirit that that is bound to bring. ... God nearly always test us through other people. ... God's will is made known in His providences,

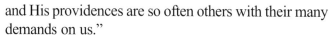

and His providences are so often others with their many demands on us."

C. Brokenness can be renewed through the c____
"If you find yourself in a patch of unbrokenness, the only way is to go afresh to Calvary and see Christ broken for you and you will come away willing to be broken for Him."
II Corinthians 5:14-15

Reflection & Application

✎What are some ways our brokennes is tested?

_____

_____

_____

Reflection & Application

✎How often can you come to the cross to have your brokennes renewed?

_____

_____

IV. The gift of His f_____

"So we get onto the Highway. There it stretches before us, a narrow uphill road, bathed in light, leading towards the Heavenly Jerusalem. The embankment on either side slopes away into thick darkness. In fact, the darkness creeps right to the very edges of the Highway, but on the Highway itself all is light"

A. "Behind us is the c____ ... no longer dark and forbidding but radiant and glowing."

B. With us is J_____, "walking the Highway overflowing with resurrection life."

"In His hands He carries a pitcher with the Water of Life. He comes right up to us and asks us to hold our our hearts, and just as if we were handing Him a cup, we present to Him our empty hearts. He looks inside–a painful scrutiny–and where He sees we have allowed His blood to cleanse them, He ills them with the Water of Life. So we go on our way rejoicing and praising God and overflowing with His new life. This is revival."

"So the rest of the Christian life simply consists now of Walking along the Highway, with hearts overflowing, bowing the neck to His will all the time , constantly trusting the blood to cleanse us and living in complete oneness with Jesus. There is nothing spectacular about this life, no emotional experiences to sigh after and wait for. It is merely the day-by-day living of the life the Lord intended us to live. This is real holiness."

V. O___ the highway

"But we may, and sometimes do, slip off the Highway, for it is narrow. One little step aside and we are off the path and in darkness."

A. S_____ off the Highway

"It is always because of a failure in obedience somewhere or a failure to be weak enough to let God do all."

> "Satan is always beside the road, shouting at us, but he cannot touch us. But we can yield to his voice by an act of the will."
> *I Peter 5:8-9*

B. G_____ back on the Highway

1. "... ask God to show what caused us to slip off"

   Psalms 139:23-24

   "... and He will, although it often takes Him time to make us see"

   I John 1:5-8

2. "As I crawl up again to the Highway on hands and knees, I come again to Him and His blood for cleansing"

   "Jesus is waiting there to fill my cup to overflowing once again. Hallelujah! No matter where you leave the Highway, you will always find Him calling you to come back and be broken again, and always the blood will be there to cleanse and make you clean. This is the great secret of the Highway–knowing what to do with sin, when sin has come in. The secret is always to take sin to the cross, see there its sinfulness, and then put it under the blood and reckon it gone.

   I John 1:9, 2:2

Reflection & Application

✎What are some of Satan's temptations which may cause you to slip off the highway?

_____

_____

_____

"So the real test along the Highway will be–are our cups running over? Have we the peace of God in our hearts? Have we love and concern for others? These things are the barometer of the Highway. If they are disturbed, then sin has crept in somewhere–self-pity, self-seeking, self-indulgence in thought or deed, sensitiveness, touchiness, self-defense, self-consciousness, shyness, reserve, worry, fear, and son."

Additional Truth

Matthew 22:37-40
37 Jesus said unto him,
Thou shalt love the Lord thy God with all thy heart,
and with all thy soul, and with all thy mind.
38 This is the first and great commandment.
39 And the second is like unto it,
Thou shalt love thy neighbour as thyself.
40 On these two commandments
hang all the law and the prophets.

VI. Our walk with o_____

"An important thing about the Highway which has not been mentioned yet is that we do not walk this Highway alone. Others walk with us."

A. The people on the Highway
   1. The L_____ Jesus
   2. Other w_____
B. The r_____ of the Highway

"... rule of the road is that fellowship with them [other wayfarers] is as important as fellowship with Jesus. Indeed, the two are intimately connected. ... Everything that comes between us and another, such as impatience, resentment, or envy, comes between us and God. ... It is clear why these two relationships should be so linked. 'God is love,' that is, love for others, and the moment we fail in love towards another, we put ourselves out of fellowship with God–for God loves him, even if we don't"

I John 4:7-11

7 Beloved, let us love one another:
for love is of God;
and every one that loveth is born of God,
and knoweth God.
8 He that loveth not knoweth not God; for God is love.
9 In this was manifested the love of God toward us,
because that God sent his only begotten Son
into the world,
that we might live through him.
10 Herein is love, not that we loved God,
but that he loved us,
and sent his Son to be the propitiation for our sins.

11 Beloved, if God so loved us,
we ought also to love one another.

"But more thant that, the effect of such sins is always to make us 'walk in darkness'–that is, to cover up and hide what we really are or what we are realy feeling. That is always the meaning of 'darkness' in Scripture, for while the light reveals, the darkness hides."

Additional Truth

John 3:19-21
19 And this is the condemnation,
that light is come into the world,
and men loved darkness rather than light,
because their deeds were evil.
20 For every one that doeth evil hateth the light,
neither cometh to the light,
lest his deeds should be reproved.
21 But he that doeth truth cometh to the light,
that his deeds may be made manifest,
that they are wrought in God.

Additional Truth

I John 2:5-11
5 But whoso keepeth his word,
in him verily is the love of God perfected:
hereby know we that we are in him.
6 He that saith he abideth in him ought himself also
so to walk, even as he walked.

Additional Truth

*7 Brethren, I write no new commandment unto you,
but an old commandment
which ye had from the beginning.
The old commandment is the word
which ye have heard from the beginning.
8 Again, a new commandment I write unto you,
which thing is true in him and in you:
because the darkness is past,
and the true light now shineth.
9 He that saith he is in the light,
and hateth his brother,
is in darkness even until now.
10 He that loveth his brother abideth in the light,
and there is none occasion of stumbling in him.
11 But he that hateth his brother is in darkness,
and walketh in darkness,
and knoweth not whither he goeth,
because that darkness hath blinded his eyes.*

"The way back into fellowship with the Lord Jesus will bring us again into fellowship with our brother, too. All unlove must be recognized as sin and given to the Lord Jesus for His blood to cover–and then it can be put right with our brother also."

"So this is the Highway life. It is no new, astounding doctrine. It is not something new for us to preach. It is quite unspectacular. It is just a life to live day by day in whatever circumstances the Lord has put us. It does not contradict what we may have read or heard about the Christian life. It just puts into simple pictorial language the great truths of sanctification. To start to live this life now will mean revival in our lives. To continue to life it will be revival continued.

49

Revival is just you and I walking along the Highway in complete oneness with the Lord Jesus and with one another, with cups continually cleansed and overflowing with the life and love of God."

The Calvary Road
Outline Guide

Chapter 5

The Dove and the Lamb

The Dove and the Lamb

"Victorious living and effective soul winning are not the product of our better selves and hard endeavors, but are simply the fruit to the Holy Spirit. We are not called upon to produce the fruit, but simply to bear it. It is all the time to be His fruit."

Additional Truth

John 15:8
8 Herein is my Father glorified,
that ye bear much fruit;
so shall ye be my disciples.

"How this may be so for us is graphically illustrated by the record, in the first chapter of John, of how the Holy Spirit came upon the Lord Jesus at His baptism. John the Baptist said of Him, 'Behold the Lamb of God, which taketh away the sin of the world,' Then as he baptized Him, he saw the heavens opened and the Spirit of God descending like a Dove and lighting upon Him."

John 1:29-36 (29, 32-36)
29 The next day John seeth Jesus coming unto him,
and saith,
Behold the Lamb of God,
which taketh away the sin of the world.
32 And John bare record, saying,
I saw the Spirit descending from heaven like a dove,
and it abode upon him.
33 And I knew him not:
but he that sent me to baptize with water,
the same said unto me,
Upon whom thou shalt see the Spirit descending,

and remaining on him,
the same is he which baptizeth with the Holy Ghost.
34 And I saw,
and bare record that this is the Son of God.
35 Again the next day after John stood,
and two of his disciples;
36 And looking upon Jesus as he walked, he saith,
Behold the Lamb of God!

I. **The h_____ of God**
   A. The L___
      "The Lamb speaks of meekness and submissiveness ..."

Additional Truth

Isaiah 53:6-8
6 All we like sheep have gone astray;
we have turned every one to his own way;
and the LORD hath laid on him the iniquity of us all.
7 He was oppressed, and he was afflicted,
yet he opened not his mouth:
he is brought as a lamb to the slaughter,
and as a sheep before her shearers is dumb,
so he openeth not his mouth.
8 He was taken from prison and from judgment:
and who shall declare his generation?
for he was cut off out of the land of the living:
for the transgression of my people was he stricken.

B. The D_____

"... the Dove of peace (what more peaceful sound than
the cooing of a dove on a summer day)."

"When the eternal God chose to reveal Himself in His son, He
gave Him the name of the Lamb; and when it was necessary
for the Holy Spirit to come into the world, He was revealed
under the emblem of the Dove."

"The main lesson of this incident is that the Holy Spirit, as the
Dove could only come upon and remain upon the Lord Jesus
because He was the Lamb. Had the Lord Jesus had any other
disposition than that of the Lamb–humility, submissiveness,
and self-surrender–the Dove could never have rested on Him.
Being herself so gentle, she would have been frightened away
had not Jesus been meek and lowly in heart."

"Here, then, we have pictured for us the condition upon which
the same Holy Spirit can come upon us and abide upon us.
The Dove can only abide upon us as we are willing to be as the
Lamb. How impossible that He should rest upon us while self
is unbroken! ... Read again in Galatians 5 the ninefold fruit of
the Spirit ... with which the Dove longs to fill us! Then
contrast it with the ugly works of the flesh ... in the same
chapter. It is the contrast of the snarling wolf with the gentle
dove"

<u>The Snarling Wolf</u>
Galatians 5:19-21
19 Now the works of the flesh are manifest,
which are these;
Adultery, fornication, uncleanness, lasciviousness,
20 Idolatry, witchcraft, hatred, variance, emulations,
wrath, strife, seditions, heresies,

21 Envyings, murders, drunkenness, revellings,
and such like:
of the which I tell you before,
as I have also told you in time past,
that they which do such things
shall not inherit the kingdom of God.

The Gentle Dove
Galatians 5:22-23
22 But the fruit of the Spirit is love, joy, peace,
longsuffering, gentleness, goodness, faith,
23 Meekness, temperance: against such there is no law.

Reflection & Application

✎Give some contrasts to how you might react to life's circumstances as a dove in comparison to a wolf?

_____

_____

_____

II.   The d_____ of the Lamb

"How clear, then that the Holy Spirit will only come upon us and remain upon us as we are willing to be as the Lamb on each point on which He will convict us!"

Additional Truth

Galatians 5:24-25
*24 And they that are Christ's have crucified the flesh
with the affections and lusts.
25 If we live in the Spirit,
let us also walk in the Spirit.*

A.   The s_____ Lamb
   John 5:19, 30
   1.   No s_____
   2.   No p_____ for helping itself
   3.   Exists in h_____
   4.   Exists in s_____

"But we–how complicated we are! What schemes we have had of helping ourselves and of getting ourselves out of difficulties. What efforts of our own we have resorted to, to live the Christina life and to do God's works, as if we were something and could do something."

B.   The s_____ lamb
   Philippians 2:5-11
   1.   Shorn of His r_____
   2.   Shorn of His r_____

3.   Shorn of His human l_____
I Peter 2:22-23

"But we–ah, we! On how many occasions have we been unwilling to be shorn of that which was our right. We were not willing for His sake to lose what was our own. We insisted, too, that we should be treated with the respect due to our position. We resisted, and we fought."

C.   The s_____ Lamb
Isaiah 53:7-8
1.   He never d_____ Himself
2.   He never e_____ Himself

"But we have been anything but silent when others have said unkind or untrue things about us. Our voices have been laud in self-defense and self-vindication, and there has been anger in our voices. We have excused ourselves, when we should have admitted frankly our wrong."

D.   The s_____ Lamb
"... there was nothing in His heart but love for those who had sent Him to the cross ... even as they were putting the nails through His hands, He was murmuring, 'I forgive you,' and He asked His Father to forgive them too."
Luke 23:33-34
1.   No r_____
2.   No g_____
3.   No b_____

"But what resentment and bitterness have not we had in our hearts–toward this one and that one, and over so much less than what they did to Jesus. Each reaction left a stain on our hearts, and the Dove had to fly away because we were not willing to bear it and forgive it for Jesus' sake."

E.   The s_____ Lamb

"The question of all questions for us just now is, 'How can the Dove return to our lives with His peace and power?' The answer is again just simply, 'The Lamb of God,' for He is not only the simply Lamb and the shorn Lamb and the silent Lamb and the spotless Lamb, But above everything else He is the substitute Lamb."

I Peter 1:18-21, Revelation 13:8

"The humility of the Lord Jesus in becoming our Lamb was necessary only that He might become on the cross our Substitute, our Scapegoat, carrying our sins in His own body on the Tree, so that there might be forgiveness for our sins and cleansing from all their stains, when we repent of them ... What a vision it is when we see these sins wounding and hurting Him now! May this solemn thought break our proud hearts in repentance! For it is only when we have seen these sins of ours in the heart of Jesus, so that we are broken and willing to repent of them and put them right, that the blood fo the Lamb cleanses us from them and the Dove returns with peace and blessing of the hearts."

> He humbled Himself to the manger,
> And even to Calvary's tree;
> But I am so proud and unwilling
> His humble disciple to be.

He yielded His will to the Father,
And chose to abide in the Light;
But I prefer wrestling to resting,
And try by myself to do right.

Lord, break me, then cleanse me and fill me
And keep me abiding in Thee;
That fellowship may be unbroken,
And thy name hallowed in me.

"Our hearts need to be broken too, and only when they are shall we be willing for the confessions, the apologies, the reconciliations and the restitutions that are involved in a true repentance of sin. Then, when we have been willing to humble ourselves, as the Lord humbled Himself, the Dove will return to us."

Return, O heavenly Dove, return,
Sweet Messenger of rest!
I Hate the sins that made Thee mourn,
And drove Thee from my breast.

"One last word. The Dove is the emblem of peace, which suggests that if the blood of Jesus has cleansed us and we are walking with the Lamb in humility, the sign of the Spirit's presence and fullness will be peace. This is indeed to be the test of our walk all the way along. 'Let the peace of God rule [arbitrate] in your hearts' (Col. 3:15). If the Dove ceases to sing in our hearts at any time, if our peace is broken, then it can only be because of sin. In some matter we have departed from the humility of the Lamb. We must ask God to show us what it is, and be quick to repent of it and bring the sin to the cross. Then the Dove will be once again in His rightful place in our hearts and peace with God will be ours. In this way we shall know that continuos abiding of the Spirit's presence which is open to even to fallen men through the immediate and constant application of the precious blood of Jesus."

Reflection & Application

✎What are some ways that you display the characteristics of a lamb in your day to day living?

_____

_____

_____

The Calvary Road
Outline Guide

Chapter 6

Revival in the Home

Revival in the Home

"Thousands of years ago, in the most beautiful garden the world has ever known, lived a man and a woman. Formed in the likeness of their Creator, they lived solely to reveal Him to His creation and to each other and thus to glorify Him every moment of the day. Humbly they accepted the position of a creature with the Creator–that of complete submission and yieldedness to His will. Be cause they always submitted their wills to His, because they lived for Him and not for themselves, they were also completely submitted to each other. Thus in that first home in that beautiful garden there was absolute harmony, peace love and oneness, not only with God but with each other."

Genesis 1:26-31

"Then one day the harmony was shattered, for the serpent stole into the God-centered home, and with him, sin. And now because they lost their peace and fellowship with God, they lost it with each other. No longer did they live for God–each lived for himself. They were each their own god now, and because they no longer lived for God they no longer lived for each other. Instead of peace, harmony, love, and oneness, there was now discord and hate–in other words, SIN!"

Genesis 3:1-13

I. Revival begins at h͟o͟m͟e͟

"It was into the home that sin first come. It is in the home that revival first needs to come ..."

A. It is the h͟a͟r͟v͟e͟s͟t͟ place

B. It is the most c͟o͟s͟t͟l͟y͟ place *seek god 1st*

C. It is the most n͟e͟c͟e͟s͟s͟a͟r͟y͟ place to begin. *cost of loss*

"But before we go on, let us remind ourselves again of what revival really is. It simply means a new life in hearts where the spiritual life has ebbed–but not a new life of self-effort or self-initiated activity. It is not man's life, but God's life, the life of Jesus filling us and flowing through us. That life is manifested in fellowship and oneness with those with whome we live–nothing between us and God, and nothing between us and others"

"All the things that come between us and other come between us and God and spoil our fellowship with Him, so that our hearts are not overflowing with divine life." *REVIVAL BRINGS CHANGE*

Additional Truth

I John 4:20-21
*20 If a man say, I love God,
and hateth his brother,
he is a liar:
for he that loveth not his brother whom he hath seen,
how can he love God whom he hath not seen?
21 And this commandment have we from him,
That he who loveth God love his brother also.*

Reflection & Application

✎Give some descriptions of a family not living in good fellowship.

PRIDE, SELFISHNESS

_____

_____

_____

II. What is w _ʀᴏɴɢ_ with our homes?

A. We are not really o _ᴘᴇɴ_ with one another

"This lack of transparency and openness is ever the result of sin ... There were reactions and thoughts in Adam's heart that Eve was never allowed to know and there were like things hidden in Eve's heart too. And so it has been ever since. Having something to hide from God, we hide it, too, from one another ... This is what the Scripture calls 'walking in darkness'–for the darkness is anything which hides."

Additional Truth

I John 2:8-11
8 Again, a new commandment I write unto you,
which thing is true in him and in you:
because the darkness is past,
and the true light now shineth.
9 He that saith he is in the light,
and hateth his brother,
is in darkness even until now.
10 He that loveth his brother abideth in the light,
and there is none occasion of stumbling in him.
11 But he that hateth his brother is in darkness,
and walketh in darkness,
and knoweth not whither he goeth,
because that darkness hath blinded his eyes.

B. We fail to really l _ᴏᴠᴇ_ one another

"Love is not just a sentimental feeling, nor even strong passion. The famous passage in 1 Corinthians 13 tells us what real love is, and if we test ourselves by it we may find that after all we are hardly loving one another at all, and our behavior is all in the opposite direction–and that opposite of love is hate!"

I Corinthians 13:4-8a
4 Charity suffereth long, and is kind;
charity envieth not;
charity vaunteth not itself, is not puffed up,
5 Doth not behave itself unseemly, seeketh not her own,
is not easily provoked, thinketh no evil;
6 Rejoiceth not in iniquity, but rejoiceth in the truth;
7 Beareth all things, believeth all things,
hopeth all things, endureth all things.
8 Charity never faileth: ...

"How do we stand up to those tests in our homes?"

Reflection & Application

✎What are some descriptions of a family that does not properly love one another?

FEAR, ANXIETY

_____

_____

Reflection & Application

✎What are some descriptions of a family that does properly love one another?

FEAR , STRIFE

_____

_____

III. The only w ay out

"Now the question is, Do I want new life, revival, in my home? I have got to challenge my heart about this. Am I prepared to continue in my present state, or am I really hungry for new life, His life, in my home?"
Psalm 51:1-19

Additional Truth

I John 1:5-10
*5 This then is the message
which we have heard of him,
and declare unto you,
that God is light, and in him is no darkness at all.
6 If we say that we have fellowship with him,
and walk in darkness, we lie, and do not the truth:
7 But if we walk in the light, as he is in the light,
we have fellowship one with another,
and the blood of Jesus Christ his Son
cleanseth us from all sin.*

Additional Truth

8 If we say that we have no sin,
we deceive ourselves, and the truth is not in us.
9 If we confess our sins,
he is faithful and just to forgive us our sins,
and to cleanse us from all unrighteousness.
10 If we say that we have not sinned,
we make him a liar, and his word is not in us.

A. Call sin s i n (my sin, not the other person's)

B. Go to the c ross with the sin
"As we bow the neck at the cross, His self-forgetful love for others, His longsuffering and forbearance flow into our hearts."

C. The precious blood will c leanse the sin
"... and the Holy Spirit fills us with the very nature of Jesus Christ."

D. Again and again we will s_____ places of sin
"... we will see places where we must yield up our rights, as Jesus yielded up His for us."

    1. "We shall have to s_____ that the thing in us that reacts so sharply to another's selfishness and pride is simply our own selfishness and pride, which we are unwilling to sacrifice."
    Ephesians 4:1-3, Galatians 5:16-26

    2. "We shall have to a ccept another's ways and doings as God's will for us and

meekly bend the neck to all God's providence"

"That does not mean that we must accept another's selfishness as God's will for him–far from it–but only as God's will for us. As far as the other is concerned, God will probably want to use us , if we are broken, to help him see his need. "Certainly, if we are parents we shall often need to correct our child with firmness. But non of this is to be from selfish motives, but only out of love for the other and a longing for his good. Our own convenience and right must all the time be yielded."

Genesis 50:15-21

E.   We must be w <u>ILLING</u> to put things right with others

"Sometimes even with the children."

Matthew 5:23-24, James 5:16

"Let us remember that at the cross there is room for only one at a time. We cannot say, 'I was wrong, but you were wrong too. You must come as well!' No, you must go alone, saying, 'I'm wrong.' God will work in the other more through your brokenness than through anything else you can do or say. We may, however, have to wait–perhaps a long time. But that should only cause us to understand more perfectly how God feels, for, as someone has said, 'He too has had to wait a long time since His great attempt to put things right with man nineteen hundred years ago, although there was no wrong on His side.' But God will surely answer our prayer and bring the other to Calvary too."

"Real oneness conjures up for us the picture of two or more sinners together a Calvary."

71

Reflection & Application

✎What are some evidences of lost peace in your life?

_____

_____

_____

*Personally make a list of the sins which you are aware of and confess each one of them to God to find His forgiveness and cleansing.

Reflection & Application

✎Are you willing to continue the process of revival in your home by asking forgiveness from those you have sinned against?

_____

The Calvary Road
Outline Guide

Chapter 7

The Mote and the Beam

The Mote and the Beam

"That friend of ours has got something in his eye! Though it is only something tiny–what Jesus called a mote–how painful it is and how helpless he is until it is removed! It is surely our part as a friend to do all we can to remove it, and how grateful he is to us when we have succeeded in doing so. We would be equally grateful to him if he did the same service for us."

"In the light of that, it seems clear that the real point of the well-known passage in Matthew 7:3-5 about the beam and the mote is not the forbidding of our trying to remove the fault in the other person, but rather the reverse.

Matthew 7:3-5

3 And why beholdest thou the mote
that is in thy brother's eye,
but considerest not the beam that is in thine own eye?
4 Or how wilt thou say to thy brother,
Let me pull out the mote out of thine eye;
and, behold, a beam is in thine own eye?
5 Thou hypocrite,
first cast out the beam out of thine own eye;
and then shalt thou see clearly
to cast out the mote out of thy brother's eye.

"We are told to 'admonish one another' [Colossians 3:15-17] and 'exhort one another,' [Hebrews 3:12-13, 10:25] to 'wash one another's feet' [John 13:12-17] and to 'provoke one another to love and good works' [Hebrews 10:24]. The love of Jesus poured out in us will make us want to help our brother in this way."

"What blessing may not come to many others through our willingness humbly to challenge one another, as led by God."

I.   What is the b ɛᴀᴍ ?

A.   The m ᴏᴛɛ - in another's eye

"It is some fault which we fancy we can discern in him; it may be an act he has done against us, or some attitude he adopts towards us."

Matthew 18:15-17, I Corinthians 6:7

Additional Truth

Matthew 5:21-22

*21 Ye have heard that it was said by them of old time,
Thou shalt not kill;
and whosoever shall kill
shall be in danger of the judgment:
22 But I say unto you,
That whosoever is angry with his brother
without a cause
shall be in danger of the judgment:
and whosoever shall say to his brother, Raca,
shall be in danger of the council:
but whosoever shall say,
Thou fool, shall be in danger of hell fire.*

B.   The bɛᴀᴍ - in our eye

"I suggest that the beam in our eye is simply our unloving reaction to the other man's mote ... The mote in him has provoked in us resentment, our coldness, our criticism, or bitterness, or evil speaking, or ill will–all of them variants of the basic ill, unlove. And that, says the Lord Jesus, is far, far worse than the tiny wrong (sometimes quite unconscious) that provoked it."

Additional Truth

I John 2:9-11
9 He that saith he is in the light,
and hateth his brother,
is in darkness even until now.
10 He that loveth his brother abideth in the light,
and there is none occasion of stumbling in him.
11 But he that hateth his brother is in darkness,
and walketh in darkness,
and knoweth not whither he goeth,
because that darkness hath blinded his eyes.

"God have mercy on us for the many times when it has been so with us and when in our hypocrisy we have tried to deal with the person's fault, when God saw there was this thing far worse in our own hearts."
*II Samuel 12:1-9

Additional Truth

Ephesians 4:31-32
31 Let all bitterness, and wrath,
and anger, and clamour, and evil speaking,
be put away from you, with all malice:
32 And be ye kind one to another,
tenderhearted, forgiving one another,
even as God for Christ's sake hath forgiven you.

"But let us not think that a beam is of necessity some violent reaction on our part. The first beginning of a resentment is a beam, as is also the first flicker of an unkind thought, or the first suggestion of unloving criticism. Where that is so, it only distorts our vision and we shall never see our brother as he really is, beloved of God. If we speak to our brother with that in our hearts, it will only provoke him to adopt the same hard attitude to us, for it is the law of human relationships that 'with what measure ye mete, it shall be measured to you again' [Mark 4:24]."

Additional Truth

Proverbs 15:1
1 A soft answer turneth away wrath:
but grievous words stir up anger.

Reflection & Application

✎What are some ways that a "beam" might be displayed in your life?

_____

_____

_____

II. Take it to C A_veR y

I John 1:6-10

A. R e s i s t _____ our unloving reaction
   Matthew 5:38-42

B. G o with it to Calvary (on our knees)
   "Get a glimpse of what our sin cost him [Jesus]"
   Isaiah 53:6-9, II Corinthians 5:21

C. R e p e n t _____ of our sin (be broken afresh)
   II Corinthians 7:8-11

D. T e l l _____ the Lord Jesus to cleanse our sin in His blood
   Psalm 51:2, 7-12

E. G o to the other individual and confess our sin and ask for forgiveness
   James 5:16

"Very often bystanders will tell us, and sometimes our own hearts, that the sin we are confessing is not nearly as bad as the other's wrong, which he is not yet confessing. But we have been to Calvary; indeed, we are learning to live under the shadow of Calvary; and we have seen our sin there and we can no longer compare our sin with another's. But as we take these simple steps of repentance, then we see clearly to cast the mote out of the other's eye, for the beam in our eye has gone ... We may see then that the mote we were so conscious of before is virtually nonexistent–it was but the projection of something that was in us. On the other hand, we may have revealed to us hidden underlying things of which our brother was hardly conscious. Than as God leads us, we must lovingly and humbly challenge him, so that he may see them too, and bring them to the fountain for sin and find deliverance."
Matthew 5:21-24, Luke 17:3-4

Additional Truth

Galatians 6:1
1 Brethren, if a man be overtaken in a fault,
ye which are spiritual,
restore such an one in the spirit of meekness;
considering thyself, lest thou also be tempted.

"When God is leading us to challenge another, let not fear hold us back. Let us not argue or press our point. Let us just say what God has told us to and leave it there. It is God's work, not ours, to cause the other to see it. It takes time to be willing to bend 'the proud stiff-necked I.' When we in turn are challenged, let us not defend ourselves and explain ourselves. Let us take it in silence, thanking the other; and then go to God about it and ask Him. If he was right, let us be humble enough to go and tell him, and praise God together."

The Calvary Road
Outline Guide

Chapter 8

Are You Willing to Be a Servant?

Are You Willing to Be a Servant?

"Nothing is clearer from the New Testament than that the Lord Jesus expects us to take the low position of servants. This is not just an extra obligation, which we may or may not assume as we please. It is the very heart of that new relationship which the disciple is to take up with respect to God and to his fellows if he is to know fellowship with Christ and any degree of holiness in his life."

Additional Truth

John 13:3-17 (3-5)
3 Jesus knowing that the Father
had given all things into his hands,
and that he was come from God, and went to God;
4 He riseth from supper,
and laid aside his garments;
and took a towel, and girded himself.
5 After that he poureth water into a bason,
and began to wash the disciples' feet,
and to wipe them with the towel
wherewith he was girded.

Additional Truth

John 13:3-17 (12-17)
12 So after he had washed their feet,
and had taken his garments, and was set down again,
he said unto them, Know ye what I have done to you?

> **Additional Truth**
>
> *13 Ye call me Master and Lord:*
> *and ye say well; for so I am.*
> *14 If I then, your Lord and Master,*
> *have washed your feet;*
> *ye also ought to wash one another's feet.*
> *15 For I have given you an example,*
> *that ye should do as I have done to you.*
> *16 Verily, verily, I say unto you,*
> *The servant is not greater than his lord;*
> *neither he that is sent greater than he that sent him.*
> *17 If ye know these things,*
> *happy are ye if ye do them.*

I. **Two types of s_____**

    A. <u>H_____</u> servants - "Who have wages paid to them and have certain rights"

    B. <u>B_____</u> servants - "Or slaves, who have no rights, who receive no wages, and who have no appeal"

> **Additional Truth**
>
> *I Corinthians 6:19-20*
> *19 What? know ye not that your body*
> *is the temple of the Holy Ghost which is in you,*
> *which ye have of God, and ye are not your own?*
> *20 For ye are bought with a price:*
> *therefore glorify God in your body, and in your spirit,*
> *which are God's.*

"When, however, we come to the New Testament, the word in the Greek for the servant of the Lord Jesus Christ is not 'hired servant,' but 'bond servant,' by which is meant to be shown that our position is one where we have no rights and no appeal, where we are the absolute property of our Master, to be treated and disposed of just as He wishes."
Romans 6:15-23, II Corinthians 5:14-15

"Further, we shall see more clearly still what our position is tobe when we understand that we are to be the bond servants of One who was Himself willing to be a bond servant. Nothing shows better the amazing humility of the Lord Jesus, who servants we are to be, than that though He was in the form of God, He 'counted it not a prize to be on an equality with God, but emptied himself, taking the form of a servant' (Phil. 2:6-7, ERV)–without rights, willing to be treated as the will of the Father and the malice of men might decree, if only He might thereby serve men and bring them back to God ... How this shows us what it means to be ruled by the Lord Jesus!"

Philippians 2:5-8
5 Let this mind be in you,
which was also in Christ Jesus:
6 Who, being in the form of God,
thought it not robbery to be equal with God:
7 But made himself of no reputation,
and took upon him the form of a servant,
and was made in the likeness of men:
8 And being found in fashion as a man,
he humbled himself, and became obedient unto death,
even the death of the cross.

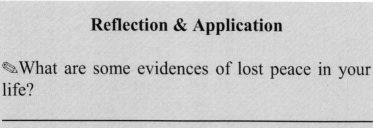

The Calvary Road - Outline Guide
Are You Willing to Be a Servant?

Reflection & Application

✎What are some evidences of lost peace in your life?

_____

_____

_____

Reflection & Application

✎What are areas of your life must you give God control of as your Lord and Master?

_____

_____

_____

II. Our servanthood to the Lord Jesus is to express itself in our servanthood to our f_____

"The low position we take toward the Lord Jesus is judged by Him by the low position we take in our relationship with our fellows. An unwillingness to serve others in costly, humbling ways He take to be an unwillingness to serve Him, and we thus put ourselves out of fellowship with Him.
Matthew 20:25-28, II Corinthians 4:6, 6:10, I John 3:16-18

86

> **Additional Truth**
>
> **Galatians 5:13**
> *13 For, brethren, ye have been called unto liberty;
> only use not liberty for an occasion to the flesh,
> but by love serve one another.*

III. The five m_____ of the bond servant

Luke 17:7-10
*7 But which of you,
having a servant plowing or feeding cattle,
will say unto him by and by,
when he is come from the field,
Go and sit down to meat?
8 And will not rather say unto him,
Make ready wherewith I may sup,
and gird thyself, and serve me,
till I have eaten and drunken;
and afterward thou shalt eat and drink?
9 Doth he thank that servant
because he did the things that were commanded him?
I trow not.
10 So likewise ye,
when ye shall have done all those things
which are commanded you,
say, We are unprofitable servants:
we have done that which was our duty to do.*

A. He must be w_____ to have one thing on top of another put upon him, without any consideration being given him.

"How unwilling we are for this! How quickly there are murmurings and bitterness in our hearts when that sort of thing is expected of us. But the moment we start murmuring, we are acting as if we had rights, and a bond servant hasn't any!"

B. He must be w_____ not to be thanked

"How often we serve others, but what self-pity we have in our hearts and how bitterly we complain that they take it as a matter of course and do not thank us for it."

C. He must not c_____ the other with selfishness

"But we? We can perhaps allow ourselves to be 'put upon' by others, and are willing perhaps not to be thanked or what we do, but how we charge the other in our minds with selfishness! But that is not the place of a bond servant. He is to find in the selfishness of others but a further opportunity to identify himself afresh with the Lord as the servant of all."

D. He must c_____ that he is an unprofitable servant

"We must confess again and gain that 'in us, that is in our flesh, there dwelleth no good thing,' [Romans 7:18] that, if we have acted thus, it is no thanks to us, whose hearts are naturally proud and stubborn, but only to the Lord Jesus, who dwells in us and who has made us willing."

E. He must a_____ that doing and bearing what he has in the way of meekness and humility, he has not done one stitch more than it was his duty to do.

"God made man in the first place simply that he might be God's bond servant. Man's sin has simply consisted in his refusal to be God's bond servant. His restoration can only be, then, a restoration to the position of a bond servant. A man, then, has not done anything specially meritorious when he has consented to take that position, for he was created and redeemed for that very thing."

"This, then, is the Way of the Cross. It is the way that God's lowly Bond Servant first trod for us, and should not we, the bond servants of the Bond Servant, tread it still? Does it seem hard and forbidding, this way down? Be assured, it is the only way up ... Those who tread this path are radiant, happy souls, overflowing with the life of their Lord. They have found 'he that humbleth himself shall be exalted' [Luke 14:11] to be true to them as for the Lord."

Additional Truth

I Peter 5:5-7
5 Likewise, ye younger,
submit yourselves unto the elder.
Yea, all of you be subject one to another,
and be clothed with humility:
for God resisteth the proud,
and giveth grace to the humble.
6 Humble yourselves therefore
under the mighty hand of God,
that he may exalt you in due time:
7 Casting all your care upon him;
for he careth for you.

Reflection & Application

✎What are some responses which may indicate that you are not acting like a bond slave to others for Jesus Christ?

_____

_____

Reflection & Application

✎What are some correct responses to the harsh treatment of others because you are a bond slave for Jesus Christ?

_____

_____

"That brings us to the all-important matter of repentance. We shall not enter into more abundant life merely by resolving that we shall be humbler in the future. There are attitudes and actions which have already taken place and are still being persisted in (if only by our unwillingness to apologize for them) that must first be repented of. The Lord Jesus did not take upon Him the form of a bond servant merely to give us an example, but that He might die for these very sins upon the cross, and open a fountain where in His precious blood they can all be washed away. But that blood cannot be applied to the sins of our proud hearts until we have been broken in repentance as to what has already happened and as to what we already are. This will mean allowing the light of God to go through every part of our hearts and into every one of our relationships. It will mean that we shall have to see that the sins of pride, which God will show us, made it necessary for Jesus to come from heaven and die on the cross that they might be forgiven. It will mean not only asking Him to forgive us be asking others too. And that will be humbling indeed. But as we crawl through the Door of the Broken Ones we shall emerge into the light and glory of the highway of holiness and humility."

Do you really deserve to have any rights?

The Calvary Road
Outline Guide

Chapter 9

The Power of the Blood of the Lamb

Jesus

BLOOD: heals

FORGIVEN

CLEANSES US

RESTORES US

MAT 11:29

JOHN 6:38 GOD'S WILL

Jesus

- didn't refuse to go
to the cross

- humble

- gave our blood.
special qualities
forgiveness of sins
+ eternal life.

- power of the lamb
Jesus was humble
as a lamb.
Most selfless animal

col 1:20 - we are reconciled before
God

The Power of the Blood of the Lamb

"The message and challenge of revival, which is coming to many of us these days, is searching in its utter simplicity. It is simply that there is only one thing in the world that can hinder the Christian's walking in victorious fellowship with God and his well being filled with the Holy Spirit–and that is sin in one form or another. There is only one thing in the world that can cleanse him from sin with all that that means of liberty and victory–and that is the power of the blood of the Lord Jesus. It is, however, most important for us that we should see what it is that gives the blood of Christ its mighty power with God on behalf of men, for then we shall understand the conditions on which its full power may be experienced in our lives."
"How many achievements and how many blessings for men the Scripture ascribes to the power of the blood of the Lord Jesus!"

- ◆ Peace is made between man and God - Colossians 1:20
- ◆ Forgiveness of sins and eternal life for all who put their faith in the Lord Jesus Christ - Colossians 1:14, John 6:54
- ◆ Satan is overcome - Revelation 12:11
- ◆ Continual cleansing from all sin for us - I John 1:7
- ◆ We may be set free from the tyranny of an evil conscience to serve the living God - Hebrews 9:14
- ◆ The most unworthy have liberty to enter the Holy of Holies of God's presence and live there all the day. - Hebrews 10:19

Lord says draw near to me I will draw near to you.

Iron sharpens Iron

X Lord point out what I need to change wash me in the blood of the lamb. Lord show me where I'm sinning.

I. Whence Its p<u>ower</u> ?

A. "The blood of the L <u>AMB</u> "

Revelation 7:14

14 And I said unto him, Sir, thou knowest.
And he said to me,
These are they which came out of great tribulation,
and have washed their robes,
and made them white in the blood of the Lamb.

"Not the blood of the Warrior, but the blood of the Lamb! In other words, that which gives the precious blood its power with God for men is the lamb-like disposition of the One who shed it and of which it is the supreme expression."

Additional Truth

Revelation 5:11-13
11 And I beheld,
and I heard the voice of many angels
round about the throne and the beasts and the elders:
and the number of them was
ten thousand times ten thousand,
and thousands of thousands;
12 Saying with a loud voice,
Worthy is the Lamb that was slain
to receive power, and riches,
and wisdom, and strength,
and honour, and glory, and blessing.

> ## Additional Truth
>
> *13 And every creature which is in heaven,*
> *and on the earth, and under the earth,*
> *and such as are in the sea,*
> *and all that are in them, heard I saying,*
> *Blessing, and honour, and glory, and power,*
> *be unto him that sitteth upon the throne,*
> *and unto the Lamb for ever and ever.*

1. His w ᴵᴸᴸ - "That of being a sacrifice for our sin"
    *John 1:29

2. His c_____ - "That He is meek and lowly in heart, gentle and unresisting, and all the time surrendering His own will to the Father's, for the blessing and saving of men"
    *Matthew 11:29
    *John 6:38

"Anyone but the Lamb would have resented and resisted the treatment men gave Him. But He, in obedience to the Father and out of love for us, did neither. Men did what they liked to Him and for our sakes He yielded all the time."

Philippians 2:5-8
5 Let this mind be in you,
which was also in Christ Jesus:

6 Who, being in the form of God,
thought it not robbery to be equal with God:
7 But made himself of no reputation,
and took upon him the form of a servant,
and was made in the likeness of men:
8 And being found in fashion as a man,
he humbled himself, and became obedient unto death,
even the death of the cross.

"How different from us!"

Isaiah 53:3-7
3 He is despised and rejected of men;
a man of sorrows, and acquainted with grief:
and we hid as it were our faces from him;
he was despised, and we esteemed him not.
4 Surely he hath borne our griefs,
and carried our sorrows:
yet we did esteem him stricken,
smitten of God, and afflicted.
5 But he was wounded for our transgressions,
he was bruised for our iniquities:
the chastisement of our peace was upon him;
and with his stripes we are healed.
6 All we like sheep have gone astray;
we have turned every one to his own way;
and the LORD hath laid on him the iniquity of us all.
7 He was oppressed, and he was afflicted,
yet he opened not his mouth:
he is brought as a lamb to the slaughter,
and as a sheep before her shearers is dumb,
so he openeth not his mouth.

"And all that to pay the price of my sin! So we see not merely is He the Lamb because He died one the cross, but He died upon the cross because He is the Lamb." "Let us ever see this disposition in the blood. Let every mention of the blood call to mind the deep humility and self-surrender of the Lamb, for it is this disposition that give the blood its wonderful power with God."

Hebrews 9:14
14 How much more shall the blood of Christ,
who through the eternal Spirit
offered himself without spot to God,
purge your conscience from dead works
to serve the living God?

"And it is this fact that bestows upon it its power with God for men. For this disposition has ever been of supreme value to God. Humility, lamb-likeness, the surrender of our wills to God, are what He looks for supremely from man. It was to manifest all this that God ever created the first man. It was his refusal to walk this path that constituted his first sin (and it has been that heart of sin ever since). It was to bring this disposition back to earth that Jesus came. It was simply because the Father saw this in Him that He could say, 'My Son, in whom I am well pleasing.' It was because the shedding of His blood so supremely expressed this disposition that it is so utterly precious to God and so all-availing for man and his sin."

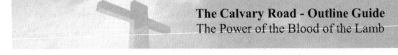
II. **How can we e_____ its full power in our lives?**
"Our hearts surely tell us the answer, as we look on the Lamb, bowing His head for us on Calvary–only ..."

    A.   By being w̲ᴜᴄ̲ʜ̲ to have the same disposition that ruled Him

       *Philippians 2:5-8, I Corinthians 2:16

    B.   By b̲ᴏ̲ᴡ̲ɪ̲ɴ̲ɢ̲ our necks in brokenness as He bowed His

       *John 19:30

       "All the fruits of the Holy Spirit, mentioned in Galatians 5–love, joy, peace, longsuffering, gentleness, goodness, faith, meekness, self control–what are they but the expressions of the lamb-like nature of the Lord Jesus with which the Holy Spirit wants to fill us? Let us never forget that the Lord Jesus, though exalted to the throne of God, is still the Lamb (the book of Revelation tells us that) and He wants to reproduce Himself in us."

Reflection & Application

✎What are some actions of an individual with a lamb like character?

MEEK, HUMBLE, FAITHFUL, CHRIST-LIKE, THE FRUIT OF THE SPIRIT UPON HIM.

100

III. Are we w_____?

"There is a hard, unyielding self, which stands up for itself and resists others, that will have to be broken if we are to be willing for the disposition of the Lamb, and if the precious blood is to reach us in cleansing power. We may pray long to be cleansed from some sin and for peace to be restored to our hearts, but unless we are willing to be broken on the point in question and be made a partaker of the Lamb's humility there nothing will happen. Every sin we ever commit is the result of the hard, unbroken self taking up the attitude of pride, and we shall not find peace through the blood until we are willing to see the source of each sin and reverse the wrong attitude that caused it by a specific repentance, which will always be humbling ... But their importance can be gauged by what it costs our pride to put them right. He may show ..."

Matthew 5:23-24
*23 Therefore if thou bring thy gift to the altar,
and there rememberest
that thy brother hath ought against thee;
24 Leave there thy gift before the altar, and go thy way;
first be reconciled to thy brother,
and then come and offer thy gift.*

A. A c_ALL_____ or apology that has to be made to someone or an act of restitution that has to be done

B. We must g_ive_ in on something and yield up our fancied rights in it (Jesus had no rights–have we then?).

C. We must g_o_ to the one who had done us a wrong and confess to him the far greater wrong

101

of resenting it (Jesus never resented anything or anyone–have we any right to?).

D.   Be o _l̲e̲n̲_ with our friends that they may know us as we really are, and thus be able to have true fellowship with us.

"These acts may well be humiliating and a complete reversal of our usual attitudes of pride and selfishness, but by such acts we shall know true brokenness and become partakers of the humility of the Lamb. As we are willing for this in each issue, the blood of the Lamb will be able to cleanse us from all sin and we shall walk with God in white, with His peace in our hearts."
*II Corinthians 4:10-11

Additional Truth

Colossians 2:6-7
6 As ye have therefore
received Christ Jesus the Lord,
so walk ye in him:
7 Rooted and built up in him,
and stablished in the faith,
as ye have been taught,
abounding therein with thanksgiving.

Reflection & Application

✎Is there an area in your life which you need to make right with God and with others so that you can experience the full power of the Blood of the Lamb and control of the Dove?

BE RE GOSPELED

The Calvary Road
Outline Guide

Chapter 10

Protesting Our Innocence?

Protesting Our Innocence?

"We have all become so used to condemning the proud self-righteous attitude of the Pharisee in the parable of the Pharisee and the Publican that we can hardly believe that the picture of him there is meant to apply to us–which only shows how much like him we really are."

Luke 18:9-14

9 And he spake this parable unto certain
which trusted in themselves that they were righteous,
and despised others:
10 Two men went up into the temple to pray;
the one a Pharisee, and the other a publican.
11 The Pharisee stood and prayed thus with himself,
God, I thank thee, that I am not as other men are,
extortioners, unjust, adulterers, or even as this publican.
12 I fast twice in the week,
I give tithes of all that I possess.
13 And the publican, standing afar off,
would not lift up so much as his eyes unto heaven,
but smote upon his breast, saying,
God be merciful to me a sinner.
14 I tell you, this man went down to his house justified
rather than the other:
for every one that exalteth himself shall be abased;
and he that humbleth himself shall be exalted.

I. **God's picture of the human h** EART
   A. Mark 7:21-22
   B. Galatians 5:19-21
   C. Jeremiah 17:9

Ephesians 4:20-24
20 But ye have not so learned Christ;
21 If so be that ye have heard him,
and have been taught by him,
as the truth is in Jesus:
22 That ye put off
concerning the former conversation
the old man,
which is corrupt according to the deceitful lusts;
23 And be renewed in the spirit of your mind;
24 And that ye put on the new man,
which after God is created in righteousness
and true holiness.

"Here then is God's picture of the human heart, the fallen self, 'the old man,' as the Scripture calls it, whether it be in the unconverted or in the keenest Christian ... The simple truth is that the only beautiful thing about the Christian is Jesus Christ. God wants us to recognize that fact as true in our experience, so that in true brokenness and self-despair we shall allow Jesus Christ to be our righteousness and holiness and all in all–and that is victory."

Reflection & Application

✎What is the true condition of your heart?

_____

_____

II.   Making God a l ᴀ៷ !

A.   Protesting y ᴏᴜʀ innocence - "living in the realm of illusion"

Luke 18:11a

11 The Pharisee stood and prayed thus with himself,
God, I thank thee, that I am not as other men are,

> "He said in effect, 'These things are doubtless true of other men–this Publican is even no confessing them–but Lord, not of me! And in so saying, he was making God a lair ...'"

I John 1:8, 10

8 If we say that we have no sin,
we deceive ourselves, and the truth is not in us.
10 If we say that we have not sinned,
we make him a liar, and his word is not in us.

> "Yet I feel sure that he was perfectly sincere in what he said. He really did believe that the was innocent of these things. Indeed, he is ascribing his imagined innocence to God, saying, 'I thank thee ...' God's Word, however still stood against him. But he just had not seen it. 'The penny had not dropped!' If the publican is beating upon his breast and confessing his sins, it is not becuae he has sinned worse than the Pharisee. It is simply that the Publican has seen that what God says in woefully true of him and the Pharisee has not ... He has not yet understood that God looks, not on the outward appearance, but on the heart ..."

I Samuel 16:7
7 But the LORD said unto Samuel,
Look not on his countenance,
or on the height of his stature;
because I have refused him:
for the LORD seeth not as man seeth;
for man looketh on the outward appearance,
but the LORD looketh on the heart.

Additional Truth

Proverbs 23:7a
7 For as he thinketh in his heart, so is he:

1.   The look of lust the equivalent of a_aDULTRY_
      - Matthew 5:27-28
2.   The attitude of resentment and hate the
      same as m_urder_ - I John 3:15
3.   Envy as actual t_____
4.   Petty tyrannies in the home as wicked as
      the most e_____ dealing in the
      market.

"Perhaps we have heard of others who have humbled
themselves and have rather despised them for the confessions
they have had to make and the things they had to put right in
their lives. Or perhaps we have been genuinely glad that they
have been blessed. But, whichever it is, we don't feel that we
have anything to be broken about ourselves. Beloved, if we
feel we are innocent and have nothing to be broken about, it is
not that these things are not there but that we have not seen

them. We have been living in the realm of illusion about ourselves."

B. Protesting o _u r__ innocence - "living in the realm of illusion"

"There is yet another error we fall into when we are not willing to recognize the truth of what God says of the human heart. Not only de we protest our own innocence, but we often protest the innocence of our loved ones ... We are living in the realm of illusion not only about ourselves, but about them too, and we fear to have it shattered. But we are only defending them against God–making God a lair on their behalf, as we do on our own, and keeping them from entering into blessing, as we do also ourselves."

"Only a deep hunger for real fellowship with God will make us willing to cry to God for His all-revealing Light and to obey it when it is given."

Additional Truth

Psalm 139:23-24
23 Search me, O God, and know my heart:
try me, and know my thoughts:
24 And see if there be any wicked way in me,
and lead me in the way everlasting.

Reflection & Application

✎Have you accepted the truth about who and what you really are in your flesh?

_____

_____

_____

III. **J**_____ **God**
   A. An admission that what God said is t R U T H
   B. An admission that God's chastening judgments are j U S T

Additional Truth

Nehemiah 9:33
*33 Howbeit thou art just
in all that is brought upon us;
for thou hast done right,
but we have done wickedly:*

"This is ever the nature of true confession of sin, true brokenness. It is the confession that my sin is not just a mistake, a slip, a something which is really foreign to my heart ("Not really like me to have such thoughts or do such thing!"), but that it is something which reveals the real 'I'; that shows me to be the proud, rotten, unclean thing God says I am; that it really is like me to have such thoughts and do such things.

It was in these terms that David confessed his sin, when he prayed ..."

Psalm 51:4
4 Against thee, thee only, have I sinned,
and done this evil in thy sight:
that thou mightest be justified when thou speakest,
and be clear when thou judgest.

"Let us not fear, then, to make such a confession where God convicts us that w must, thinking that it will 'let Jesus down.' Rather, the reverse is true, for out of such confession God gets glory, for we declare Him to be right. This brings us to a new experience of victory in Christ, for it declares afresh that 'in me (that is, in my flesh) dwelleth no good thing,' [Romans 7:18] and brings us to a place where we give up trying to make our incorrigible selves holy and where we take Jesus to be our holiness and His life to be our life."

Reflection & Application

✎Will you accept God's description of what you are and admit that you deserve His judgement?

IV. Peace and C CLEANSING

"But the Publican did something more than justify God. He pointed to the sacrifice on the altar, and found peace with God and cleansing from sin as he did so. That comes out in the literal meaning of the words which he uttered, 'God be merciful to me, a sinner.' In the Greek the words mean literally, 'God be propitiated to me the sinner.' The only way by which a jew knew that god could be propitiated was by a sacrifice, and, in all probability, at that very hour the lamb for the daily burnt offering was being offered up on the alter in the temple."

"A man never comes to this position of brokennes but that God shows him the Divine Lamb on Calvary's cross, putting away his sin by the shedding of His blood. The God who declares beforehand what we are provides beforehand for our sin."

Additional Truth

I Peter 1:18-21

*18 Forasmuch as ye know that ye were not redeemed
with corruptible things, as silver and gold,
from your vain conversation
received by tradition from your fathers;
19 But with the precious blood of Christ,
as of a lamb without blemish and without spot:
20 Who verily was foreordained
before the foundation of the world,
but was manifest in these last times for you,
21 Who by him do believe in God,
that raised him up from the dead,
and gave him glory;
that your faith and hope might be in God.*

"In Him, who bore them in meekness, my sins are finished. And as I, in true brokenness, confess them, and put my faith in His blood, they are cleansed and gone. Peace with God then comes into my heart, fellowship with God is immediately restored, and I walk with Him in white."

"As we walk with Him in the Light, He will be showing us all the time the beginnings of things which, if allowed to pass, will grieve Him and check the flow of His life in us–things which are the expression of that old proud self for which God has nothing but judgment ..."

Additional Truth

Psalm 119:105
*105 Thy word is a lamp unto my feet,
and a light unto my path.*

Additional Truth

Psalm 43:3
*3 O send out thy light and thy truth:
let them lead me;
let them bring me unto thy holy hill,
and to thy tabernacles.*

"But Such are the ones, God says, who 'dwell with Him in the high and holy place,' [Isaiah 57:15] and who experience continuous revival"

Additional Truth

Psalm 27:1, 4

1 The LORD is my light and my salvation;
whom shall I fear?
The LORD is the strength of my life;
of whom shall I be afraid?
4 One thing have I desired of the LORD,
that will I seek after;
that I may dwell in the house of the LORD
all the days of my life,
to behold the beauty of the LORD,
and to enquire in his temple.

Additional Truth

Psalm 15:1-5

1 LORD, who shall abide in thy tabernacle?
who shall dwell in thy holy hill?
2 He that walketh uprightly, and worketh
righteousness,
and speaketh the truth in his heart.
3 He that backbiteth not with his tongue,
nor doeth evil to his neighbour,
nor taketh up a reproach against his neighbour.
4 In whose eyes a vile person is contemned;
but he honoureth them that fear the LORD.
He that sweareth to his own hurt, and changeth not.
5 He that putteth not out his money to usury,
nor taketh reward against the innocent.
He that doeth these things shall never be moved.

"There then is our choice–to protest our innocence and go down to our house unblessed, dry of soul, and out of touch with God. Or to justify God and to enter into peace, fellowship, and victory through the blood of Jesus."

Reflection & Application

✎Will you make a decision now to continually return to the Cross of Jesus Christ to remember the payment and power of His blood for your life?

_____

Other Ministry Resources Available
From
Walking in the WORD Ministries
www.walkinginthewordministries.net

Marriage: A Covenant Before God presents 10 biblical studies about marriage, each one is based on the marital relationship of Adam and Eve and has the purpose of helping young couples understand God's plan and purpose for their life together. Included are practical questions, illustrations, and applications for each biblical truth in order that the couple might grow in their knowledge of each other and how they can glorify God together.

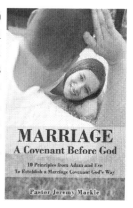

Parenting with Purpose seeks to help young parents to spiritually prepare for the great privilege they have to care for and guide the life of one of God's precious creations. The first three lessons focus on the parents' need to honor God with their child, while the final three lessons focus on the parents' opportunity to represent God the Father to their child.

Missions: Ministering Beyond Our Borders was written to provide insight into the physical, emotional, and spiritual adjustments a missionary faces as he begins his new life and ministry. Throughout its pages you will find spiritual encouragements for the missionary and helpful hints for his family and friends who desire to support him in his service to their Lord and Savior Jesus Christ. There is also "Missionary Edition" which provides a large appendix with additional tips specifically for missionaries.

The Deputation Trail: Ministry or a Means to an End? was written to help missionaries during their pre-field ministry by presenting biblically-based philosophies and practical tips to guide them through a God-honoring, church-expanding, and believer-edifying, deputation ministry.

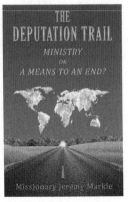

Made in the USA
Middletown, DE
20 August 2018